Cookie
Bouquets

Create Your Own Gifts & Centerpieces

Delicious Designs

Printed in the United States of America
by G&R Publishing Co.

Published By:

CQProducts

507 Industrial Street
Waverly, IA 50677

ISBN-13: 978-1-56383-300-7
ISBN-10: 1-56383-300-X
Item #3623

Table of Contents

Getting Started

These great-looking bouquets make the perfect gift or party decoration – and they are deliciously sweet too! Use the no-fail recipes beginning on page 56 for easy and beautiful centerpieces. You may also use your own favorite recipes or ready-to-use refrigerated cookie dough and icings. However, follow these tips for best results:

- Reduce or omit baking powder from your cut-out cookie dough recipes to achieve clean cuts and nice edges.
- Press down on tops of hot baked cookies with a flat spatula to create a flat surface for decorating.
- If using refrigerated sugar cookie dough, blend some powdered sugar into it before rolling out on a surface covered with additional powdered sugar, instead of flour.
- Always make a few extra cookies in case of breakage or decorating mistakes. This allows you to add more cookies to your container as needed to achieve a nice full appearance.

Make every bouquet unique by interchanging the suggested types of cookies and icings. For example, make the sports bouquet with iced brownies instead of peanut butter cookies or make the Patriotic Salute with frosted gingerbread cookies instead of sugar cookies. The only limit is your imagination!

Gather Some General Supplies

These supplies may be purchased in kitchen shops, grocery stores or the baking section of discount stores.

- Food-safe containers (at least 3″ deep)
- Florist foam or Styrofoam ("foam")
- Knife to trim foam
- Scissors and decorative scissors
- Tape
- Waxed paper and aluminum foil
- Colored tissue paper
- Nonstick cooking spray
- Quart-size, heavy-duty zippered plastic bags
- Lollipop and cookie sticks (4″, 6″, 8″)
- Wood popsicle or craft sticks (4½″)
- Bamboo skewers (12″)
- Toothpicks
- Food coloring (Gel or paste coloring is recommended for the best color and consistency.)
- Ready-to-use decorating frostings and icings in plastic tubes and/or bottles: writing icing, writing gel, white cookie icing, black and red decorating icing
- Bent icing knife

Preparing the Base

Choosing a fun container to enhance your bouquet theme is an important part of your cookie creation. Be sure it is food-safe and heavy enough to support the weight of cookies on stems without tipping over. It should be at least 3″ deep with a wide opening for easy assembly. Choose colors, ribbons and trims that enhance the colors used on your cookies. Thrift stores, craft stores and your own closets are great places to find the perfect container.

In some bouquets, crisp cereal treats are pressed into the bottom of a lined container to hold the stems. After the cookies are removed, you can enjoy the edible base.

In other bouquets, non-edible Styrofoam is used. The foam should fit into the container snugly. To cut foam to the correct size, press the container's opening against the foam to make an outline. Use a knife to cut out the shape, approximately ½″ inside the outline. Test the fit; trim foam as needed, angling cuts so foam fits down into container, about ½″ below top edge. Wrap foam with aluminum foil and then proceed as directed in the bouquet instructions. Colorful tissue paper or shredded paper is often used to cover the foil. Tuck tissue edges down into container with a craft stick.

Plan your arrangements based on the type and size of your container and your cookie cutters. Use the photos for ideas, then make the bouquets your own by choosing stem lengths and placements that work for your products.

Choosing and Attaching Flower Stems

Wood craft sticks and white paper-style lollipop or cookie sticks are inserted into cookie dough shapes *before* baking. The sticks should extend about halfway up each cookie. Once cookies are baked and cooled, these stems should support the cookies securely. Brownies, cupcakes and no-bake cookies will be prepared first and sticks will be inserted after shaping. A good rule of thumb is that the heavier the cookie, the sturdier and shorter the stick needs to be.

In forward-facing bouquets, cookies placed near the front of an arrangement need shorter sticks. Those in the back need longer sticks. Lollipop sticks that are too long may be cut or broken off to the desired length. If in doubt about your arrangement, start with longer sticks (6″ or 8″) and trim them when putting the bouquet together. Adjust cookies so bouquet is well-balanced.

When inserting stick stems into the base, handle them *underneath* the cookie. Push stems down firmly and slowly, stopping to check depth and appearance of arrangement. Push them far enough to obtain good support. Do not push stems all the way down until you are sure about placement. It is hard to undo a deep hole. If necessary, make a starter hole with a toothpick. To adjust cookie positions, handle cookies by unfrosted edges so frosting remains intact.

This bright "flower" bouquet
contains twelve Oreo cookies,
covered with colored cellophane.

You will need:

- **Styrofoam**
- **Container (Sample uses a footed vase, 3½″ deep and 4″ in diameter.)**
- **Ribbons (Sample uses narrow pink, purple and blue ribbons to match cellophane.)**
- **Double Stuf Oreo cookies**
- **Foil**
- **Bamboo skewers**
- **Colored cellophane (Sample uses pink, purple and blue.)**
- **Green cellophane**
- **Chenille stems to match all cellophane, including green**

To Begin...

1 Prepare the container.

Cut foam to fit snugly into container. Cover with foil and green cellophane. Press covered foam into container at least ½″ below top rim. Tie ribbons around base of container if desired.

2 Cover cookies with foil.

• Cut a 4″ square of foil for each cookie. Wrap cookies in foil, pressing foil against front of cookie with fingers so cookie pattern shows.

• Gently push point of skewer through foil and into creamy filling at one edge of each cookie, about 1″ to 1½″.

3 Cut cellophane and chenille stems.

• Cut an 8″ square paper pattern. Trace pattern and cut one 8″ cellophane square for each flower, using a variety of colors.

• Make an oval paper pattern, 5 x 4 ½″. Trace pattern and cut two green cellophane ovals for each flower.

• Cut a 2″ piece of matching chenille stem for each flower.

• Cut a 6″ piece of green chenille stem for each flower.

4 Wrap cookies in cellophane.

• Place each cookie on the center of a cellophane square and fold top diagonally over cookie. Pleat top edges and fold toward stem on front and back sides as shown. With fingers, gather cellophane tightly just below cookie.

• Tightly wrap a 2″ matching chenille stem around cellophane and skewer two times and twist ends. Pull cellophane edges back around cookie.

5 Add cellophane leaves.

• Use a skewer point to poke a hole in the center of two green cellophane ovals. Slide ovals onto flower stem, up to cookie. Turn ovals so they are offset. Press ovals against cookie and gather all layers of cellophane tightly.

• Wrap end of green chenille stem tightly around gathered cellophane, twisting it twice. Wrap remaining green stem around skewer until secure. Fluff green "leaves".

6 Put bouquet together.

Push skewers into foam in container, arranging colors and blossoms as desired. Start in front and work toward the back. Break off skewers as needed to get a variety of flower heights, with tallest flowers at the back. If needed, poke starter holes into foam with a toothpick before inserting skewers.

Try these variations:

- Make a dozen "red roses" by wrapping all cookies in red cellophane.
- Wrap long green chenille stems around length of each skewer, if desired.
- The flower arrangement can face one direction, as shown in sample, or flowers can be arranged in a dome shape so bouquet is attractive from all sides.

This balloon bouquet contains
a dozen chocolate chip cookies
covered in colored cellophane
and tied with narrow ribbon.

You will need:

- Container (Sample uses a painted metal pail, 5″ deep and 6″ in diameter.)
- Styrofoam
- Blue tissue paper
- White fiberfill
- Chocolate chip cookies, prepared from an 18 oz. tube refrigerated dough or your favorite recipe
- White lollipop sticks (4″ and 6″)
- Colored cellophane (Sample uses pink, blue, yellow, orange, purple and green.)
- Narrow ribbon to match cellophane, cut into 12″ pieces
- White paint marker
- Colored craft wire (24 gauge)

To Begin...

1 Prepare container. Cut foam to fit snugly into container. Cover foam with foil and blue tissue paper. Tuck covered foam down into container and arrange fiberfill over tissue-covered foam.

2 Bake cookies. *If using refrigerated chocolate chip cookie dough:* Cut refrigerated dough into ½″ slices. Use hands to shape slices to resemble balloon shapes. *If using homemade chocolate chip cookie dough:* Use hands to shape each heaping spoonful of dough into a balloon shape about ½″ thick.

Transfer shapes to ungreased baking sheet and insert a lollipop stick into bottom of each balloon about 1″ to 1½″. Bake as directed, about 9 to 13 minutes, or until golden brown. Cool on baking sheet for 2 to 3 minutes, then move cookies to waxed paper to cool completely.

3 Wrap cookies in cellophane.

• Use a sheet of 8½ x 11″ paper for a pattern. Trace around pattern and cut one cellophane rectangle for each balloon you will make. (Sample has one blue, two purple, two yellow, two pink, two orange and three green balloons.)

• Place a cookie face down on one piece of cellophane, with top of cookie 4½″ from top edge of cellophane and ½″ from side edge, as shown.

• Repeatedly fold cellophane lengthwise around cookie creating a double layer of cellophane on the front side. Tape edge down on back of cookie.

• Fold top edges of cellophane toward center twice, then fold top down over back of cookie so end extends past bottom of cookie. Gather all cellophane together just below cookie. Wrap ribbon around gathered cellophane.

- Tie ribbon tightly into a knot, then tie a small bow.
- Trim cellophane to about ½″ below ribbon.
- If desired, print "Happy Birthday", "Congratulations", "Get Well" or another appropriate greeting on the front of one or more balloons with the paint marker. Let paint dry.

4 Put bouquet together.

Plan your arrangement of balloons. They may be arranged with taller balloons toward the back and shorter ones in front or placed randomly around the center, as if balloons are free-flying. Gently move aside fiberfill and firmly push sticks into foam. Don't push on tops of cookies.

5 Add finishing touches.

Cut wire into 10″ to 14″ lengths. Coil each wire around a marker or pen leaving about 3″ straight. Gently push straight wire end into foam, arranging wires as desired among balloons. Adjust bows and fiberfill as necessary. If desired, add curled ribbon strands to edges of container or as a table decoration around the bouquet.

Berry Sweet Buds

Berry Sweet Buds

Crispy treats made with berry-
flavored cereal form the base
and buds for this bouquet.
The buds are covered with vanilla
candy coating in a variety of colors.

You will need:

- Container (Sample uses a round footed dish, about 3″ deep and 4″ in diameter.)
- Crisp Berry Treats (recipe on page 60)
- Microwavable vanilla candy coating (or white almond bark)
- Gel food coloring (yellow, orange, red)
- White lollipop sticks (4″ and 6″)
- Green craft foam

To Begin...

1 Prepare crisp cereal treats and container. Prepare one batch of Crisp Berry Treats using recipe on page 60. Spray container with nonstick cooking spray. Firmly press a portion of the crispy treats into the container, almost even with the top edge. (If the container is deeper than 3″, place a small piece of foil-wrapped foam in the bottom first. Place waxed paper over the top, coat with nonstick spray and press cereal mixture on top of that.)

2 Form flower buds. Use remaining crispy treats to create flower buds. Use your hands to mold a ball of cereal mixture around one lollipop stick. Press firmly to make "bud" shapes that cling to stick, slightly pointed on top and rounded at the bottom. Make about eight buds on 6″ sticks and 15 buds on 4″ sticks. Refrigerate for 10 minutes.

3 Coat buds with melted vanilla candy coating.

• Follow package instructions to melt about 10 ounces of vanilla candy coating in a microwave until smooth and creamy.

• Divide melted coating between two bowls. Add yellow food coloring to one bowl until color reaches desired intensity. Holding one bud over the bowl, spoon melted yellow coating over bud, turning bud and swirling coating as desired until well covered. Leave a small amount of cereal exposed on top of some buds. Tap off excess coating on the side of bowl.

• Set stem end into Styrofoam to dry. Repeat to make three or four yellow buds.

• Add orange food coloring to remaining yellow candy coating; stir and reheat as needed to make a peach color. Spoon melted peach-colored coating over several buds.

• To remaining white candy coating, add red food coloring to make light pink. Reheat as needed to melt coating. Cover several buds with pink coating.

• Add more red food coloring to remaining pink to make a darker shade of pink. Coat several more buds.

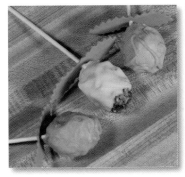

• To use any excess melted coating, drizzle a thin line of contrasting color over several buds in a wavy pattern with a small spoon.

• If desired, leave a few buds uncoated.

4 **Cut green foam leaves and assemble flowers.**
Using an enlarged version of the pattern below, cut out a green foam leaf for each flower, using plain or decorative scissors. Poke a hole in the middle of each leaf shape with a toothpick. Slide a leaf shape onto each flower stem and push up to the bottom of bud.

leaf pattern

├─────── 2″ ───────┤

5 **Arrange flower buds in container.**
• Push stems into crispy treat mixture in container, arranging coated flowers in container first. Break off stems as needed to get a variety of heights so arrangement looks nice from all sides. Fill in the open spaces with remaining uncoated buds, handling gently so stems do not poke through tops of buds.
• Any extra buds can be tied together with bright ribbon and displayed or eaten!

Blooms & Butterflies

Give a bunch of colorfully iced
sugar cookie flowers and butterflies
to brighten someone's day.

You will need:

- **Container (Sample uses a ceramic pot 5″ deep and 5″ in diameter.)**
- **Styrofoam**
- **Green tissue paper**
- **Never-Fail Sugar Cookie Dough (recipe on page 56)**
- **Shiny Icing (recipe on page 59)**
- **Gel food coloring (yellow, orange, red, violet, blue, green)**
- **Cookie cutters (flowers in various sizes and shapes, 2″, 3″, 3½″; 2″ butterfly)**
- **White lollipop sticks (4″ and 6″)**
- **Green craft wire (24 gauge)**
- **Skittles candies**

To Begin...

1 **Prepare container.** Cut foam to fit snugly into container. Wrap foam in foil and cover with green tissue paper. Place into container, on a bed of crumpled foil, so top of foam is ½″ below top of container.

2 **Prepare cookies.** Prepare Never-Fail Sugar Cookie Dough using recipe on page 56. You will need a partial batch for this bouquet; use remaining dough for another bouquet. Roll out dough to about ¼″ thickness.

- With cookie cutters, cut matching pairs of cookies in these shapes: five large flowers; one or two medium flowers; four small flowers; two or three butterflies. Place one cookie of each pair on ungreased baking sheets, allowing space between cookies for the sticks.

- Place one stick on each cookie, with end just past the middle. Set matching cookie on top, lining up edges. Lightly press cookies together.

- Bake at 350° for 8 to 12 minutes. Remove from oven and let cool on baking sheets for several minutes; transfer to waxed paper to cool completely.

3 Prepare and apply icing.

Prepare one batch of Shiny Icing using clear vanilla extract using recipe on page 59.

- Divide icing between six small bowls. You will need 1 to 2 generous teaspoons of icing for each large flower or for piped details.

- Add red food coloring to one bowl. Spread red icing on one large and one small flower; set aside remaining red icing for centers.

- Spread plain white icing on one medium flower. Spoon a small amount of red icing on center of white flower. Use a toothpick to drag red icing toward flower petals. Place colored sprinkles in center while icing is wet; let dry.

- Add orange food coloring to one bowl; stir well. Spread orange icing on two large and three small flowers; let dry.

- Add yellow food coloring to another bowl; stir well. Spread yellow icing on one large flower and over top and edges of one butterfly; let dry.

- Add blue food coloring to another bowl. Spread blue icing over top and edges of one butterfly; let dry.

- Spoon a small circle of contrasting icing on centers of flowers as desired. Be sure base coat of icing is completely dry before decorating with additional icing.

4 Add details.
Thicken remaining icing with a little powdered sugar; stir well to achieve a piping consistency.

• Place each color into a separate plastic bag as directed for piping on page 60. Pipe designs on butterflies and flowers, such as outlines, swirls and dots. See photos for examples.

5 Add wire leaves.
Cut a piece of green wire for each flower, 8″ to 12″ long. Twist wire tightly around stem of each flower two or three times. Curl wire ends by coiling wire around a pencil or lollipop stick. Bend "leaves" up or down as desired.

6 Put bouquet together.
Plan flower placement and press stems through tissue into foam, making starter holes with a toothpick as needed. Scatter candies around base of flowers over tissue to complete bouquet.

Flower Garden

This colorful cupcake flower garden contains 15 miniature and standard size frosted cupcakes in a chocolate cereal base that is edible too!

You will need:

- Container (Sample uses a 5 x 9" wood and metal basket, 3½" deep.)
- 1 (18.25 oz. or 9 oz.) pkg. cake mix (Sample uses strawberry flavor.)
- Eggs, oil and water as directed on package
- Crisp Chocolate Treats (recipe on page 60)
- Buttercream Frosting (recipe on page 59)
- Gel food coloring (pink, blue, yellow)
- Small round sprinkles

To Begin...

1 Prepare cupcakes.
Line two miniature cupcake pans and one regular cupcake pan with paper liners. Mix cake mix according to package instructions. Fill each lined muffin cup ⅔ to ¾ full of batter. Bake miniature cupcakes 8 to 11 minutes or until a toothpick inserted in middle comes out clean. Bake regular cupcakes for 18 to 22 minutes or as directed on package. Cool cupcakes on wire rack.

2 Prepare container and cereal base.
Line container with waxed paper and spray with nonstick cooking spray. Prepare one batch of Crisp Chocolate Treats following the recipe on page 60. Press cereal mixture into container very firmly. Chill for 30 minutes. Trim off top edge of waxed paper with scissors, making it even with top of cereal mixture. Lift it out of container while trimming, if necessary.

3 Prepare and tint frosting.

Prepare one batch of Buttercream Frosting using clear vanilla extract using recipe on page 59.

• Divide frosting between four small bowls. Three will be tinted; one will remain white.

• Add pink food coloring to one bowl; mix well.

• Add blue food coloring to one bowl; mix well.

• Add yellow food coloring to one bowl; mix well.

• Spread a thin coat of each colored frosting over tops of three miniature cupcakes and one regular cupcake.

• Slightly thicken and spoon each colored frosting into a plastic zippered bag as directed for piping on page 60. For two-tone flowers, add a heaping tablespoonful of white frosting into each bag, next to the colored frosting as shown above. Use hands to push frostings together toward the bag's corner. Clip a ¼″ to ⅜″ diagonal slice off the corner of each bag.

4 Pipe flowers on cupcakes.

• Practice on waxed paper before making flowers on cupcake. Starting at the center of a cupcake, squeeze frosting out of bag, making a ribbon loop as shown. Continue around cupcake, turning as needed to make even loops.

• Make a second layer of shorter loops on top, with a rounded mound in center.

• Place small colored sprinkles on the center of each flower while frosting is soft. Press them gently in place with a toothpick.

• Place decorated cupcakes on a pan in refrigerator for 5 to 10 minutes to set frosting.

5 Put bouquet together.

Set flower cupcakes on the cereal "dirt" base in container to resemble a flower garden. Arrange them with small flowers around edges, tipping outward, and large cupcakes in the middle.

Variation: Cupcake Flowers on Stems

• Chill cereal mixture in chosen container thoroughly. Accordion fold a 2 x 7″ piece of green cellophane for each flower. Apply 2½″ of double-sided tape down the middle of folded cellophane. Wrap sticky part around a craft stick twice, 1″ to 1½″ from end, to make leaves. Cut cellophane ends at an angle to make leaves about 1½″ long; fluff out. After decorating cupcake flowers, poke a starter hole in the paper liner at one side of each cupcake. Gently push craft stick stem into hole with cellophane leaf just below flower. Push sticks into the cereal base, arranging flowers as desired.

• If preferred, omit cereal mixture base and use a foam base covered in foil and brown tissue paper. Add a sprinkling of dry chocolate crisp cereal on top of tissue to resemble dirt.

Celebrate a special girl's birthday
with this bouquet of sugar cookie
crowns and wands.

You will need:

- Container (Sample uses a round wire basket, 3″ deep and 7″ in diameter.)
- Pink netted ribbon, 3″ wide
- Styrofoam
- Pink cellophane
- Never-Fail or Holiday Sugar Cookie Dough (recipe on page 56 or 57)
- Cookie cutters (5″ crown; small and medium stars, 2½″ and 3½″; 3″ to 4″ oval or square shape)
- White lollipop sticks (4″ or 6″) or craft sticks (4½″)
- Buttercream Frosting (recipe on page 59)
- Gel food coloring (pink, violet)
- Colored sugar (pink, violet)
- Edible white glitter
- French pearl dragees (size #5 oyster pearls)
- Multi-colored sprinkles (jumbo rainbow nonpareils)
- Other party sprinkles: daisies, dots, strips, etc.
- Narrow ribbons (pink, lavender, white and/or silver)
- Optional: white ready-to-use cookie icing

To Begin...

1 **Prepare container.** Weave ribbon through side of basket and tie a bow in front; trim ends. Cut foam to fit container; cover foam with foil. Cut pink cellophane large enough to wrap around foam; tape it on bottom side. Cut a second piece of pink cellophane, 4″ larger than foam on all sides. Set taped side of foam on center of cellophane piece and press both into container with cellophane edges standing up. Fold edges toward center to make a cellophane ruffle, tucking it between foam and container with a craft stick.

2 Prepare cookies.

You will need a partial batch of sugar cookie dough; use remaining dough for another bouquet. Roll out dough to a thickness of ⅜″ to ½″.

- Cut these shapes with cookie cutters: four crowns, two medium stars; three to five small stars; one oval or square. Place shapes on ungreased baking sheets, allowing space between cookies for the sticks.

- Slide two 6″ lollipop sticks or one craft stick into the bottom of each crown, with ends just past the middle. Use lollipop sticks in varying lengths for each star. No sticks are needed for the oval or square "sign".

- Bake at 350° for 8 to 12 minutes. Remove from oven and let cool on baking sheets for several minutes; transfer to waxed paper to cool completely.

3 Prepare and apply frosting.

Prepare one batch of Buttercream Frosting with clear vanilla extract using recipe on page 59.

- Divide frosting between three small bowls.

- Spread plain white frosting on one crown and one small star. Decorate as desired.

- Add pink food coloring to one bowl; stir well. Spread pink frosting on two crowns, one medium star, one or two small stars, and the sign. Decorate with colored sugar, dragees and sprinkles.

- Add violet food coloring to remaining bowl; stir well. Spread lavender frosting on one crown, one medium star and two small stars. Decorate as desired.

4 **Add piped details.** Thicken and prepare desired color(s) of icing for piping as directed on page 60. Pipe the party girl's name on one crown. Pipe "Princess" or "Queen for a Day" on the oval or square cookie. Add outlines, swirls and dots as desired.

5 **Tie ribbons on wands.** Cut ribbons into 8″ to 10″ lengths. Tie ribbons tightly around stems of star cookies to create "wands". Trim ribbon ends to 2″ or 3″ lengths. Push knots up on stems, near bottom of cookies.

6 **Put bouquet together.** Plan arrangement using photo as a guide. Poke small starter holes into foam through cellophane with a toothpick. Place crown cookies first, followed by wands. Insert stems into foam, pressing down gently but firmly. Prop sign in front of arrangement.

Tips

- Children can decorate their own crown and wand because the buttercream frosting stays soft long enough to press in dragees or other decorations.
- For quick lettering, use ready-to-use white icing or writing gel. Print each guest's name on a crown.
- Frosting may be softened in the microwave for a few seconds for easier spreading.

Enjoy the beach any time
of the year with this bouquet of
brightly-iced sugar cookies.

You will need:

- **Container (Sample uses a painted metal bucket, 5½″ deep and 6″ in diameter.)**
- **Styrofoam, optional**
- **Crisp Rice Cereal Treats (recipe on page 60)**
- **2 graham crackers**
- **Never-Fail Sugar Cookie Dough (recipe on page 56)**
- **Cookie cutters (small, medium and large circles, 1¾″, 2½″ and 3¾″; 3½″ palm tree; 4″ ice cream cone; 3½″ fish; 3¾″ foot)**
- **Lollipop sticks (4″, 6″ and 8″)**
- **Shiny Icing (recipe on page 59)**
- **Gel food coloring (yellow, red, blue, orange, green, violet)**
- **Multi-colored sprinkles**
- **Black writing gel or decorating icing**

To Begin...

1 Prepare container and cereal base.
• If your container is deep, like the sample, cut a foam piece, 2″ to 3″ thick, to fit bottom of container. Wrap foam in foil and place into container. Then line container with waxed paper, extending it up the sides. Spray waxed paper with nonstick cooking spray.

• Prepare ½ batch (or full batch if container is large) of Crisp Rice Cereal Treats using recipe on page 60. Press cereal mixture firmly into lined container for the base. Crush graham crackers; sprinkle crumbs on top of cereal to represent sand. Refrigerate for 30 minutes.

2 Prepare cookies.
You will need a partial batch of Never-Fail Sugar Cookie Dough (recipe on page 56); use remaining dough for another bouquet. Roll out dough to a thickness of ⅜″ to ½″.

• Cut these shapes with cookie cutters: one large circle (sun); two medium circles (beach balls); one small circle (balloon); two ice cream cones; two palm trees; one fish; two footprints. Turn one foot-shaped cookie over to create a right and left footprint. Place shapes on ungreased baking sheets, allowing space between cookies for the sticks.

31

- Slide an 8″ lollipop stick into the bottom of sun and balloon cookies. Slide a 6″ lollipop stick into the bottom of each tree and ice cream cone. Slide a 4″ lollipop stick into each beach ball and fish. Footprints do not need sticks. See photos on pages 30 and 33 for examples.

- Bake at 350° for 8 to 12 minutes. Remove from oven and let cool on baking sheets for several minutes; transfer to waxed paper to cool completely.

3 Prepare and apply frosting.

Mix one batch of Shiny Icing with clear vanilla extract using recipe on page 59.

- Divide icing between four small bowls.

- Add blue food coloring to one bowl; stir well. Spread blue icing on balloon. Add more blue food coloring to bowl and stir. Spread a small blue triangle on one or both beach balls, using a toothpick to spread into corners, as shown; let dry.

- Add yellow food coloring to one bowl; stir well. Spread yellow icing on sun, fish and top of one ice cream cone.

Spread a small yellow triangle on each beach ball; let dry.

- Add a little red food coloring to third bowl; stir well. Spread pink icing on top of remaining ice cream cone. Top with candy sprinkles while icing is wet; let dry.

- Add a dot of orange food coloring to remaining pink icing in bowl to achieve a peach color. Spread this on each footprint, leaving a narrow rim of cookie unfrosted; let dry.

- Thicken and prepare remaining white icing for piping, as directed on page 60. Set aside until step 4*.

- Mix a second batch of Shiny Icing (if needed) using clear vanilla extract.

- Place about 2 tablespoons of icing in one bowl. Add green food coloring; spread green icing on top of each tree. Spread a small green triangle on beach ball(s); let dry.

- Place 3 to 4 tablespoons of icing into another bowl. Add orange food coloring. Spread two wavy orange stripes on the yellow fish. Spread a small orange triangle on each beach ball; let dry.

- To remaining orange icing, add a dot of violet food coloring and mix to make light brown. Spread brown icing on tree trunks and cones below ice cream; let dry.
- Add red food coloring to some of remaining white icing. Spread a small red triangle on each beach ball; let dry. Make a red "cherry" on top of one ice cream cone.
- Add violet food coloring to remaining white icing. Spread a small purple triangle on each beach ball; let dry.

4 **Add piped details.** Use photo below as a design guide.

- Add a dot of black food coloring to brown icing in bowl; mix well to make dark brown. Thicken and prepare dark brown icing for piping, as directed on page 60. Pipe dark brown cross-hatches on each tree trunk.

- Use white piping icing in plastic bag from step 3* on page 32. Pipe a white reflection line on balloon. Pipe white cross-hatches on each brown cone. Pipe white zigzag lines around sun. Pipe white lines between colors on beach balls and a large dot where colors meet. Pipe a white eyeball on the fish.

- Use black gel or icing to outline the orange stripes on fish and add a black dot to the fish eye. Draw black sunglasses, smile and eyebrows on the sun. Outline both feet in black. Let all icing details dry.

5 **Put bouquet together.** Plan arrangement using photo as a guide. Push sticks into the cereal base, starting at the back with the tall sun and working toward the front. Push sticks down into foam, if needed, for better support. Place one or both footprints on the "sand" at the front. After removing the cookies, cut and serve the cereal treats too.

Patriotic Salute

Patriotic
Salute

Combine iced heart and star sugar
cookies with an eagle Oreo and
marshmallow confection for
a tasty tribute to freedom.

You will need:

- Container (Sample uses a ceramic canister, 6″ deep and 5″ in diameter.)
- Styrofoam
- White tissue paper
- Red shredded paper
- Red and white ribbon (1″ wide)
- Holiday Sugar Cookie Dough (recipe on page 57)
- Shiny Icing (recipe on page 59)
- Cookie cutters (small and medium stars, 2″ and 3½″; small, medium and large hearts: 2″, 3″ and 4″; 4″ oval; 3″ bell)
- Gel food coloring (red, blue, yellow, orange, black)
- Bamboo skewer
- White lollipop sticks (4″ and 6″)
- Star sprinkles
- 1 to 2 oz. microwavable chocolate and vanilla candy coating (or almond bark)
- 1 Double-Stuf Oreo cookie
- 1 regular marshmallow
- 2 T. shredded coconut
- 1 cashew nut
- 2 miniature chocolate chips
- Ready-to-use icing (red, white, blue, black)

To Begin...

1 Prepare container.
Cut foam to fit into container snugly; wrap with foil and press into container. Cover top with white tissue paper and scatter red shredded paper on top. Tie ribbon around container as shown. Set aside.

2 Prepare cookies.
Mix one batch of Holiday Sugar Cookie Dough using recipe on page 57. Roll out dough to a thickness of ⅜″ to ½″.

- Cut these shapes with cookie cutters: two large hearts; one medium heart; six small hearts; five to eight small stars; three large stars; one oval shape (sign); one bell. Place on ungreased baking sheets, allowing space between cookies for the sticks.

- Omit sticks on five small stars, two small hearts and the oval sign.

- Slide a 4″ lollipop stick into the bottom of two small hearts and one small star. Slide a 6″ lollipop stick into the bottom of each remaining cookie.

- Bake at 350° for 8 to 12 minutes. Remove from oven and let cool on baking sheets for several minutes; transfer to waxed paper to cool completely.

3 Prepare and apply frosting.

Mix one batch of Shiny Icing with clear vanilla extract using recipe on page 59.

• Spread white icing over top and edges of each small star on a fork, tapping fork on bowl so excess icing drips back into bowl. Set stars on waxed paper, sliding them with a toothpick to a fresh space after 5 minutes if icing puddles around edges. When icing is dry to the touch, pick up stars and pat edges smooth as needed.

• Spread white icing on one large heart and two large stars, leaving a narrow edge unfrosted; let dry.

• Place 1 to 2 teaspoons of icing in a small bowl. Add yellow food coloring and mix well. Spread yellow icing on bell cookie; let dry.

• Place 2 to 3 tablespoons of icing into another bowl. Add blue food coloring. Spread blue icing on oval sign, one large star and two small hearts; let dry.

• Add red food coloring with a bit of orange to remaining icing in bowl. Spread red icing on one small, medium and large heart; let dry.

• Drizzle red icing over top and sides of two small hearts, moving on waxed paper as directed above. When icing is dry to the touch, pick up stars and pat edges smooth; let dry.

4 Assemble cookies and add piped details.

• Attach a small red heart cookie to the large white heart with a bit of white icing, as shown.

• Attach a small white star cookie to red heart with a bit of white icing.

• Thicken remaining white, blue and red icings for piping, as directed on page 60, or use prepared icings in tubes.

• Use white piping to print "USA" (or other words) on blue oval sign and draw wavy lines on a medium red heart. Make a white star on a blue heart.

• Use a drop of matching piping to attach star sprinkles to cookies as desired.

- Use black icing to draw a "crack" on the yellow Liberty bell.

- Use blue and red piping to draw lines on several white stars. Add red or blue dots or stars at the ends of wavy lines. Let all icing details dry.

5 Make 1 eagle cookie.

- Firmly twist the point of a bamboo skewer into the center of a flat side of an Oreo cookie.

- Melt chocolate candy coating in microwave for 40 seconds or until melted and smooth. Coat cookie with melted chocolate; push skewer into foam to dry.

- Place coconut on a plate; crush with hands to make fine pieces.

- Melt vanilla candy coating in microwave for 40 seconds or until melted and smooth. Stick a toothpick into one end of marshmallow. Coat marshmallow with melted vanilla coating. Immediately roll sides and top in coconut, leaving bottom uncovered. Remove toothpick and set marshmallow bottom on chocolate-covered cookie; hold for 10 seconds or until set.

- Make a toothpick hole in the side of marshmallow for beak. Dip large end of cashew into melted vanilla coating. Press cashew into hole until set.

- Make small toothpick holes for the eyes. Dip pointed end of chocolate chips into melted vanilla coating and press each chip in place for eyes until set.

6 Put bouquet together.

Plan arrangement, using photo as a guide. Push sticks into foam base, starting with eagle at the back of arrangement and working toward the front. Prop sign against front cookie. Set white stars and red hearts around edges with frosted sides facing forward.

Play Ball!

Sports fans will enjoy these peanut butter cookies with buttercream frosting. Celebrate a variety of sports, or make all cookies to represent a single sport.

You will need:

- **Container (Sample uses a 5 x 5″ box, about 7½″ deep.)**
- **Styrofoam**
- **Red tissue paper**
- **White shredded paper**
- **White and blue ribbon (1½″ wide)**
- **Peanut Butter Cookie Dough (recipe on page 56)**
- **Open cookie cutters (small, medium and large circles, 1¾″, 2″, 2⅝″; 4″ football; 3″ star; 4″ baseball cap; 3½″ football helmet; 5″ triangle*)**
- **White lollipop sticks (6″ and 8″)**
- **Buttercream Frosting (recipe on page 59)**
- **Round white sprinkles**
- **Gel food coloring (yellow, orange, black, blue)**
- **Unsweetened cocoa powder**
- **Ready-to-use writing or decorating icing (white, black, red)**

To Begin...

1 Prepare the container.
Cut foam to fit into container snugly. Wrap it in foil. Place into container and cover top with red tissue paper. Tie ribbon around top of box or attach bow to front.

2 Prepare cookies.
Prepare Peanut Butter Cookie Dough using recipe on page 56. You will need a partial batch for this bouquet; use remaining dough for another bouquet.

• To make cookie shapes, place cookie cutters on baking sheet. Roll a piece of dough in sugar, set it into cookie cutter and press dough to a thickness of ⅜″. Make these shapes: two small circles; one medium circle; two large circles; one football; one star; one helmet; one cap; one triangle pennant*. Leave space for sticks.

*If triangle cookie cutter isn't available, cut a paper triangle for a pennant pattern, 5″ long and 3½″ at side edge. Shape dough with hands using the pattern on top as a guide.

- Slide 6″ sticks into the bottom of both small circles and pennant just past the middle. Slide 8″ sticks into remaining cookies.
- Bake at 350° for 8 to 10 minutes or until lightly browned. Remove from oven and press tops of each cookie with a metal spatula to flatten surface. Let cool on baking sheets for several minutes; transfer to waxed paper to cool completely.
- If desired, use a pizza cutter to trim off edges of pennant cookie to make a sharp triangle while cookie is still warm.

3 Prepare and tint frosting.

Mix one batch of Buttercream Frosting using recipe on page 59.

- Spread white frosting on one small circle (golf ball), one medium circle (baseball), one large circle (soccer ball), pennant and football helmet, using a bent icing knife to make surface very smooth. While frosting is still soft, press round white sprinkles into small ball to look like dimples in golf ball; let dry.
- Divide remaining frosting between four small bowls.
- Add orange food coloring to one bowl; mix well. Spread orange frosting on one large circle (basketball); let dry.
- Add yellow food coloring to one bowl; mix well. Spread yellow frosting on one small circle (tennis ball) and star; let dry.
- Add blue food coloring to one bowl; mix well. Spread blue frosting on the cap; let dry.
- Thicken remaining blue frosting and place into plastic bag for piping as directed on page 60. Set aside.
- Mix 2 tablespoons of cocoa powder into remaining bowl; stir well. Spread brown frosting on football; let dry.

4 Add piped details, using the photos as guides.

• Use white icing to pipe lines and a letter on blue baseball cap. Draw white lines on brown football and yellow tennis ball.

• Use black icing to pipe lines on soccer ball and outline the star. Print a name on the star as desired.

• Use red icing to pipe stitching lines on baseball and outline the football helmet. Write a slogan on the pennant and add red details to baseball cap as desired.

• Use blue piping in plastic bag to outline pennant and add lettering to football helmet. Let all icing details dry.

5 Put bouquet together.

Beginning at the back side, push tallest stems into foam. Place shortest cookies at the front, using photo as a placement guide.

Variation:

To assemble a baseball bouquet, decorate two or more baseball cookies and use a matching baseball cap and pennant in the arrangement.

Sweet Deal

This arrangement of iced
chocolate brownies is perfect for
game players. It's best to prepare the
brownies the day before assembly.

You will need:

- Container (Sample uses a 7″ round wood box, about 3″ deep.)
- Styrofoam
- Playing cards
- Low-temperature glue gun
- Red or green tissue paper
- 1 (19.5 oz.) pkg. fudge brownie mix
- Oil, eggs and water as directed on package
- Open cookie cutters (diamond, heart, spade, club, each 3″ to 4″; 1¾″ circle)
- Shiny Icing (recipe on page 59)
- Craft sticks or thick cookie sticks (6″)
- Ready-to-use writing or decorating icing (red, black, blue, green)

To Begin...

1 Prepare the container.

• Cut foam to fit snugly into container. Wrap foam with foil and place into container.

• Arrange playing cards and glue them to side of container, overlapping and tilting them in different directions.

• Use scissors to trim cards even with bottom and top edges of container.

• Cover top of foil with tissue paper, tucking it in as needed.

2 Prepare brownies.

Prepare and bake brownies in a 9 x 13" pan as directed on package. Do not under-bake. Cool completely.

• Use cookie cutters to cut out brownie shapes, pressing cutter firmly to bottom of pan. Cut one heart, one diamond, one club, one spade and three circles. Remove from pan with a spatula.

• Make a paper pattern for the die as shown below. Set the paper pattern on brownies and cut around it with a plastic knife. Remove from pan.

2"   *die pattern*

2"

• Turn brownie shapes bottom side up and place on waxed paper. Press down on all brownies lightly to compact them slightly.

3 Decorate brownies.

Mix one batch of Shiny Icing with clear vanilla extract using recipe on page 59.

• Spread white icing on each brownie shape, stopping ¼" from outer edge. Let icing dry.

• Place a writing tip on a tube of black icing. Outline the die with black. Draw the inside lines and dots as shown in photo; let dry.

• Place a star tip on the black icing. Outline the club and spade shapes with a thick line of black, along unfrosted border; let dry.

• Place a star tip on a tube of red icing. Outline the heart and diamond shapes with a thick line of red, along unfrosted border; let dry.

• Place a writing tip on the red icing. Outline one of the circles. Add lines and inner circle to resemble a poker chip, as shown; let dry.

• Use green and blue writing icing (or a tube with a writing tip) to make two more poker chips; let dry.

• Break one cookie stick in half. Gently push one piece of stick into the bottom of the red poker chip.

• Break one craft stick in half. Gently push craft stick half into bottom of die.

• Gently push full cookie stick into bottom of blue poker chip. Remaining shapes do not need sticks.

• Place brownies into a loosely covered container and let them stand overnight.

4 **Put bouquet together the next day.**
Plan your arrangement, using photo as a guide. Make starter holes in foam with toothpick, if needed. Gently push the stick with blue poker chip into foam at the back of arrangement*. Push die stick in next. Place spade, diamond, club and heart shapes in container as shown, with shapes stacked and overlapping slightly. Place remaining poker chips as desired.

Tip:

---

*You may prefer to remove brownies from sticks, place sticks into foam as desired and then replace brownies on sticks as shown above.

This bouquet contains 16 iced gingerbread cookies ranging in size from small to large — perfect for Autumn!

You will need:

- **Gingerbread Cookie Dough (recipe on page 57)**
- **Cookie cutters (3″ circle; 3½″ mitten; small, medium and large pumpkins, 3″, 4″ and 5″; small acorn; 3½″ football; 4″ leaf)**
- **White lollipop sticks (4″ and 6″)**
- **Styrofoam**
- **Container (Sample uses a 7 x 9″ oval basket, 3″ deep, with autumn ribbon tied around.)**
- **Yellow tissue paper**
- **Shiny Icing (recipe on page 59)**
- **Gel food coloring (orange, red, yellow, violet, green)**
- **Small colored candies or multi-colored jumbo sprinkles**
- **Candy corn**

To Begin…

1 Prepare cookies.

Prepare one batch of Gingerbread Cookie Dough using recipe on page 57. Roll out dough to a thickness of ⅜″ to ½″.

- Cut these shapes with cookie cutters: one circle; two mittens; one of each pumpkin size; two to three acorns;

two footballs; five or six leaves. Place cookie shapes on ungreased baking sheets, allowing space between cookies for sticks. Turn one mitten over to make a left and right "hand" when baked.

• Turn the football shapes into ears of Indian corn. With the edge of a craft stick, draw indented lines to make corn leaves, as shown. Use a knife to cut away part of the leaf shape and round off the top of the ear of corn.

- Slide two 4″ sticks into bottom of scarecrow's head (large circle). Slide one 4″ stick into the bottom of each mitten and pumpkin. Slide a 6″ stick into at least three of the leaves and 4″ sticks into remaining leaves, placing them at various spots so some leaves will be upside down, like falling leaves. Slide a 4″ stick into the bottom of each Indian corn.
- Bake at 350° for 8 to 12 minutes. Remove from oven and let cool on baking sheets for several minutes; transfer to waxed paper to cool completely.

2 Prepare container.

Cut foam to fit snugly into container. Wrap foam in foil and cover with yellow tissue paper; place into container.

3 Prepare and apply icing.

Mix one batch of Shiny Icing with brown vanilla extract using recipe on page 59.

- Divide icing between two bowls. Add orange food coloring to one bowl; stir well. Spread orange icing on all pumpkins and one leaf; let dry.
- Add yellow food coloring to remaining icing; stir well. Spread yellow icing on two leaves; let dry.
- Add red food coloring to remaining yellow icing. Spread this darker orange color on two or three leaves; let dry. If a still-darker shade of orange is desired, add a dot of black and mix well; spread on a leaf.
- Mix a second batch of Shiny Icing with brown vanilla extract to get an off-white shade.
- Spread off-white icing on large circle and left and right mittens. Let dry.
- Transfer half of remaining off-white icing to another small bowl; cover and set aside.
- Add a dot of yellow and violet food coloring to remaining icing; mix well. Add a dot of orange food coloring and mix to achieve a light brown or khaki color. Spread khaki icing on the leaves of both ears of corn.

4 Prepare and apply piped icing.

• Thicken khaki icing for piping, as directed on page 60. Spoon mixture into a plastic bag. Cut off a tiny piece from the corner. Use khaki piping to outline unfrosted acorn. Add cross-hatch details as shown in photo below.

• Using photo below as a guide, pipe khaki cords and bows around mittens. Pipe "straw hair" on top of scarecrow's head. Outline corn leaves.

• Divide remaining off-white icing between two small bowls. Add orange food coloring to one bowl and stir well. Thicken orange icing for piping, as directed on page 60. Pipe orange lines on each leaf to look like veins, as shown. Outline pumpkins and pipe crease lines on them.

• Add green food coloring to remaining off-white icing. Thicken for piping as directed on page 60. Fill in pumpkin stems with green piping. Pipe a green twirling "vine" on each pumpkin.

5 Add details.

With a toothpick, spread a bit of remaining khaki icing on "kernel" part of Indian corn. Thin with a drop of water, if necessary. While icing is wet, press small candies randomly in place for kernels, using yellow, red, orange and purple candies. Let all icing details dry.

6 Put bouquet together.

Plan arrangement using photo as a guide. Push sticks firmly into foam, making starter holes with toothpick, if needed. (Place scarecrow head and mittens before filling in with leaves.) Sprinkle candy corn over base.

Enjoy the view and then feast
on this winter scene made
with crispy cereal treats
covered in candy coating.

You will need:

- **Container (Sample uses a 7″ square metal tin, 3″ deep.)**
- **Styrofoam**
- **Crisp Rice Cereal Treats (recipe on page 60)**
- **Lollipop sticks (white and/or green, 4″ and 6″)**
- **Microwavable vanilla candy coating (or white almond bark)**
- **White edible glitter, optional**
- **Gel food coloring (green)**
- **Microwavable chocolate candy coating (or chocolate bark)**
- **Ready-to-use white cookie icing**
- **Miniature round candies (1 orange and other colors)**
- **Ribbon (¼″ and ½″)**
- **Black writing gel or decorating icing**
- **1 round pretzel**
- **Starburst candies**

To Begin...

1 Prepare container and crisp cereal treats.
- Cut foam to fit container; wrap in foil and place in bottom of container. Line container with waxed paper, extending it up the sides. Spray waxed paper with nonstick cooking spray; set aside.
- Prepare one batch of Crisp Rice Cereal Treats using recipe on page 60. Press about two-thirds of mixture into lined container over wrapped foam, or until just below top edge of container. Set aside.

---

2 Form trees, snowman and snowballs from remaining crispy treat mixture.
- *For trees:* Cut a paper triangle pattern about 4″ tall and 3″ at wide end; set aside. Spray a piece of waxed paper with nonstick cooking spray. Spoon remaining crisp cereal mixture onto waxed paper and use hands to form a 7 x 8″ rectangle, about 1″ thick. Place tree pattern on top and use a sharp knife to cut out five cereal triangles. Set aside.

• *For snowman and snowballs*: Roll remaining scraps of cereal mixture into three small graduated balls. Put together to make a small snowman. Roll three to five tiny balls (½″ to ¾″ in diameter) for a pile of snowballs.

3 Coat cereal mixture with melted candy coating.

• *For container*: Follow package instructions to melt 4 ounces of vanilla candy coating in a microwave oven until smooth and creamy. Spread over cereal mixture in tin until evenly coated. Sprinkle with white edible glitter, if desired.

• *For trees*: Melt 6 ounces of vanilla candy coating until smooth and creamy. Stir in green food coloring. Place a tree triangle on a slotted spatula over bowl and spoon green coating over top and sides, spreading to cover.

Tap spatula on side of bowl to remove excess coating. Set on waxed paper. Repeat with two more trees.

• Make two chocolate trees in the same way, using 4 ounces of melted chocolate candy coating. Refrigerate trees for 10 minutes or until set.

• Remove trees from refrigerator and turn them over on fresh waxed paper. Slide a lollipop stick into the bottom of each tree, 1″ to 2″, using a 4″ stick in each chocolate tree and a 6″ stick in each green tree. Spread matching melted coating on the back of each tree; refrigerate until set.

• *For snowman and snowballs*: Melt 2 ounces of vanilla candy coating until smooth. Poke a toothpick into the snowman's head and body; spoon melted coating over snowman and set on waxed paper. While coating is still wet, press a tiny orange ball into snowman's head for a "carrot" nose. Dip snowballs in melted coating and place on waxed paper to dry.

4 Add details.

• *For trees*: Squeeze a thin line of white cookie icing back and forth across the front of each tree as shown. Press on small candies as desired; let dry.

• Tie narrow ribbon around chocolate tree stems.

• *For snowman*: Use black writing gel or decorating icing to make dot eyes and mouth on snowman's head; let dry. Break a round pretzel in half; push one end of each "arm" into sides of the middle ball.

5 Prepare gifts and scarf.

• *Gifts*: Use white icing to draw ribbons and bows on unwrapped Starburst candies. For a larger gift, push two candies together and cover seam with icing ribbon. If desired, add candies. Let dry.

- *Scarf*: Heat an unwrapped Starbust candy in the microwave for 12 seconds. Use hands to flatten, stretch and roll it into a scarf, 6″ to 7″ long. Flatten ends and cut with a sharp knife to resemble fringe. Wrap scarf around snowman's neck.

6 Put bouquet together.

- Use the photo for a placement guide. Press tree sticks into the cereal base as shown.

- Press a short piece of toothpick into the bottom of one gift. Press other end of toothpick into snowman's tummy, moving his arms to look like he's holding the gift. Press half a toothpick into bottom of snowman and set him in place, pressing toothpick down into base.

- Make a stack of gifts and a pile of snowballs, using a drop of icing to hold them in place as needed. If desired, tie ribbon around top of container, making a bow in front.

Variation

Candy gifts and "lights" on tree may be omitted. Add additional snowmen if desired.

Frosting the Snowman

1 **Prepare sugar cookies.**
Prepare, cut and bake the following cookies:
- 1 (4″) circle on a 4″ stick
- 1 (4″) circle on a 6″ stick
- 2 mittens on 6″ sticks (turning one over to make a right and left hand)
- 4 to 6 (3″) snowflakes on 6″ sticks
- 2 (1″) circles without sticks

2 **Prepare container.**
Cut and place foil-covered foam in container. Tuck white tulle around edges, pushing it down between container and foam with a craft stick.

3 **Decorate cookies with Shiny Icing when cool.**
Spread white icing on both large circles and two snowflakes. Sprinkle with edible glitter; let dry. Divide remaining icing into two bowls. Add a bit of blue food coloring to one bowl; stir well. Spread light blue icing on two snowflakes. Add more blue food coloring to the same bowl; stir well. Spread darker blue icing on two snowflakes. Mix red food coloring into remaining bowl. Spread red icing on mittens. Add blue food coloring to red icing in bowl for a dark purple color. Thicken slightly with powdered sugar and place into bag. Pipe a purple zigzag line on each mitten as shown. Draw purple buttons on snowman's body. Using black gel or icing, fill in 1″ circle cookies. Draw snowman's eyes and mouth on head circle with black icing. Mix yellow and red writing icing to make orange. With a toothpick, draw a carrot nose on snowman's face. Attach ear muffs (black circles) to snowman's head as shown with white icing; press to hold. Bend 4″ black chenille stem into a half circle. Attach ends of stem to head cookie above ear muffs with a dot of white icing. Pipe white icing snowflakes on mittens; let all icing details dry.

4 **Put bouquet together.**
Place body cookie near center front of container, with cookie close to base. Place head in back, peeking above body. Place mittens on each side of body, slightly behind. Place three or four snowflakes in back, showing above snowman's head. Place one or two snowflakes low in front, cutting stems shorter as needed.

Peanut Butter Cookies
Makes about 24 cookies

½ C. margarine, softened
⅓ C. peanut butter
½ C. sugar
½ C. brown sugar
1 tsp. vanilla extract

1 egg
1¾ C. flour
½ tsp. baking soda
½ tsp. salt
Additional sugar

Preheat oven to 350°. In a large mixing bowl, cream margarine and peanut butter on medium speed until well blended. Add sugar and brown sugar; beat well. Add vanilla and egg, beating until light and fluffy. Add flour, baking soda and salt; mix until well blended. Place some sugar in a small bowl. Roll a spoonful of dough in sugar. Place open cookie cutter on baking sheet. Use fingers to press dough into cookie cutter to about ⅜″ thickness. Remove cutter. Flatten top of cookie slightly with fingers. Insert a lollipop stick into bottom of each cookie, twisting it gently to keep stick inside dough. Sticks should be inserted 1″ to 1½″. Bake for 8 to 10 minutes or until lightly browned. Remove from oven and flatten tops gently with a metal spatula. Cool on baking sheet for 2 minutes before removing cookies to waxed paper to cool completely.

Never-Fail Sugar Cookies
Makes about 36 cookies

This dough holds its shape well when cut. It is wonderful for cookie cutters with small details because the cookies will not spread out during baking.

1 C. butter, softened
1 C. sugar
1 egg
1 tsp. vanilla extract

3 C. flour
1 tsp. baking powder
¾ tsp. salt

In a large mixing bowl, cream butter and sugar on medium speed until fluffy. Beat in egg and vanilla until well blended. In a separate bowl, stir together flour, baking powder and salt. Add dry ingredients to creamed mixture, a little at a time, and beat until dough is well mixed and comes together. If desired, divide dough into 2 or 3 portions and shape each one into a flat disk. Cover and chill for 1 to 2 hours before rolling out. Then follow cutting and baking instructions on page 58.

Holiday Sugar Cookies
Makes about 24 cookies

Because this recipe contains some brown sugar, these tasty cookies will have a slightly darker color, but will also hold their shape well with detailed cookie cutters.

½ C. butter, softened
¼ C. sugar
3 T. brown sugar
1 egg
1 tsp. almond extract

1½ C. flour
¾ tsp. ground cardamom, optional
¼ tsp. salt

In a medium mixing bowl, cream butter and sugars on medium speed until fluffy. Beat in egg and almond extract until well blended. In a separate bowl, stir together flour, cardamom and salt. Add dry ingredients to creamed mixture, a little at a time, and beat until dough is well mixed. Shape dough into a 1″ thick flat disk. Wrap and chill for 1 hour before rolling out. Then follow cutting and baking instructions on page 58.

Gingerbread Cookies
Makes about 24 cookies

⅔ C. shortening
1 C. sugar
1 egg
¼ C. molasses
½ tsp. baking soda

2 C. flour
1 tsp. salt
1 tsp. ground cinnamon
1 tsp. ground ginger
1 tsp. ground cloves

In a large mixing bowl, cream shortening and sugar on medium speed until fluffy. Beat in egg and molasses until well blended. In a separate bowl, stir together baking soda, flour, salt, cinnamon, ginger and cloves. Add dry ingredients to creamed mixture, a little at a time, and beat until dough is well mixed. Cover bowl and chill for 1 to 2 hours before rolling out. Then follow cutting and baking instructions on page 58. After removing cookies from oven, flatten tops gently with a metal spatula.

General Cutting, Baking and Stem Instructions for all Cut-Out Cookies

Preheat oven to 350°. Roll one portion of dough to a thickness of ¼" to ½" on a lightly floured surface*. Thickness will depend on style of bouquet being made; see bouquet instructions. Cut into desired shapes and space cookies evenly on an ungreased shiny baking sheet, leaving room for the sticks. Insert a lollipop stick into one edge of each cookie, twisting it gently to keep stick inside dough. Sticks should be inserted 1" to 1½". (Larger or heavier cookies may need two sticks for good support.) Bake for 8 to 12 minutes. Adjust time for thicker cookies as they may need to bake longer. Cool cookies on baking sheet for 2 to 3 minutes before removing to waxed paper to cool completely.

If using tubes of refrigerated cookie dough, work some powdered sugar into dough with hands. Then sprinkle work surface and rolling pin generously with additional powdered sugar in place of flour.

Rolling Tips

- Divide dough into portions which are easy to handle.

- Chilled dough is much easier to roll out. Form portion of dough into a round disk before rolling out on a lightly floured board. Handle one portion at a time, refrigerating other portions until ready to use.

- Roll out cookie dough effortlessly by taping a large piece of floured canvas to the countertop. Cover a wooden rolling pin with a cloth pastry sleeve and flour it before rolling dough.

- For a no-stick, no-flour method of rolling, place disks of soft dough between two pieces of parchment paper and roll them out to the desired thickness. Then refrigerate the rolled dough on the paper for about 20 minutes. When chilled, peel off paper and cut the cookies.

- After cutting out cookie shapes, remove excess dough and set it aside. Do all first rollings and cuttings, then combine dough scraps to reroll and cut additional shapes. Cookies get slightly drier and tougher with each re-rolling.

- When cutting very large cookie shapes, roll and cut dough directly on the baking sheet, then remove scraps. This prevents shape distortion when cookies are moved from the cutting surface to a baking sheet.

Recipe and Baking Tips

- If using your own favorite sugar cookie recipe, eliminate or cut back on the baking powder for cleaner cuts and details.
- If cookies puff up during baking, gently press the tops of hot cookies with a smooth metal spatula to make the cookie surface smooth and flat for decorating.
- For best results, remove sugar cookies from oven after they are done but before they begin to brown.
- Dough can be frozen. Or, dough can be rolled, cut and frozen to be baked later. Or, cookies can be cut, baked and frozen before frosting.
- For even baking, place cookies of similar size and thickness on the same baking sheet.

Shiny Icing
Decorates 9 to 10 large cookies

This icing goes on smoothly and dries shiny to a light touch in about 20 minutes.

1 C. powdered sugar	1½ T. milk (or orange juice)
¼ tsp. clear vanilla extract (or brown vanilla for "muddier" colors)	

In a small bowl, combine powdered sugar, vanilla and milk, a little at a time; stir until well blended, smooth and shiny. Spoon on center of cookie and spread to edges with the back of a spoon, bent icing knife or toothpick.

Buttercream Frosting
Decorates 8 to 10 large cookies and 5 to 6 small cookies

This is a good recipe to use with children helpers. It stays soft longer so decorative sprinkles can be applied easily.

¼ C. white shortening	2 C. powdered sugar
¼ C. butter, softened	1 to 1½ T. milk
½ tsp. clear vanilla extract (or brown vanilla for "muddier" colors)	

In a large mixing bowl, cream shortening and butter on medium speed. Add vanilla; mix well. Add powdered sugar, one cup at a time, beating well after each addition. Scrape bowl often. Add milk and beat until light and fluffy. Keep bowl covered with a damp cloth until ready to use. Store any leftover frosting in an airtight container in the refrigerator for up to 2 weeks. Beat again before using. Spread with a bent icing knife.

To make Chocolate Buttercream Frosting:
Stir in ⅓ cup unsweetened cocoa powder with the vanilla. Add 1½ to 3 additional teaspoons of milk as needed to achieve a good spreading consistency.

To Apply Icing or Frosting

Use a bent icing knife or spoon to nudge icing or frosting toward edges of cookies. A toothpick can be used to move it into small areas. Be sure base coat of icing or frosting is completely dry before applying contrasting details, to avoid bleeding colors.

To Pipe on Icing or Frosting

Thicken icing or frosting by adding more powdered sugar, one spoonful at a time. Mix well. Spoon thickened icing or frosting into one corner of a quart-size heavy-duty zippered plastic bag. Push mixture down into corner. Snip off a small piece of the corner with scissors. Twist bag above the icing and squeeze evenly to pipe frosting out of the hole in bag. Be sure base icing is dry to the touch before piping on details.

Glazing Cookies

To seal unfrosted cookies before decorating and keep them fresh for up to two weeks, brush baked, cooled cookies with a glaze. Mix ⅓ cup powdered sugar, 1 teaspoon light corn syrup and 2 teaspoons warm water. Stir well and brush glaze on one side of cookies. Let dry on waxed paper for 1 hour. Turn cookies over and brush second side. Let dry completely before storing or decorating. Glazed cookies can be frozen in an airtight container and decorated later.

Crisp Rice Cereal Treats

Full Recipe:

¼ C. margarine
40 regular marshmallows
   (10 oz. pkg.)
8½ C. crisp rice cereal

Half Recipe:

2 T. margarine
20 regular marshmallows
4¼ C. crisp rice cereal

In a large nonstick saucepan over medium heat, melt margarine. Add marshmallows, heat and stir until mixture is melted and smooth. Add cereal and stir until well coated. Press into containers as directed.

To make Crisp Berry Treats:
Substitute berry-flavored crisp cereal pebbles for crisp rice cereal.

To make Crisp Chocolate Treats:
Substitute cocoa-flavored crisp cereal pebbles for crisp rice cereal.